Fun with Ramen Noodles

Publications International, Ltd.

Pictured on the front cover (from left top): Chicken Nuggets with Spicy Tomato Dipping Sauce *(page 14)*, Ramen "Spaghetti" Tacos *(page 83)*, Open-Faced "S'Mores" *(page 90)*, and Cheesy Italian Noodle Bake *(page 36)*.

Pictured on the back cover (clockwise from left top): 7-Layer Dip *(page 10)*, Coconut Shrimp *(page 12)*, Broccoli Slaw *(page 21)*, Stuffed Bell Peppers *(page 50)*, Apricot Beef with Sesame Noodles *(page 64)*, Ramen Pizza Pie *(page 76)*, Glazed Noodle Crunch *(page 92)*, Ramen Pepperoni & Cheese Casserole *(page 78)*, Asian Ramen Noodle Soup *(page 70)*, Denver Quiche *(page 42)*, and Mandarin Salad *(page 35)*.

ISBN-13: 978-1-4508-4919-7
ISBN-10: 1-4508-4919-9

Manufactured in China.

8 7 6 5 4 3 2 1

Microwave Cooking: Microwave ovens vary in wattage. Use the cooking times as guidelines and check for doneness before adding more time.

Publications
International, Ltd.

Contents

Simple Starters

Timesaving Thai Wraps

- 1   package (3 ounces) chicken-flavored ramen noodles*
- 2   teaspoons creamy peanut butter
- 1½   cups packaged coleslaw mix
- ½   cup diced cooked chicken
- 8   (6-inch) flour tortillas
-       Soy sauce (optional)

*Discard seasoning packet.

1 Cook noodles according to package directions; do not drain. Add peanut butter, one teaspoon at a time, stirring until melted. Stir in coleslaw mix and chicken; cover and set aside 2 minutes.

2 Spoon noodle mixture onto tortillas. Sprinkle with soy sauce, if desired. Wrap and serve immediately.

Makes 8 wraps

 Tip:

These small wraps make a great appetizer or light snack.

Western Ramen Frittata

1 package (3 ounces) chicken ramen noodles, broken into chunks

8 eggs

1 cup shelled edamame, thawed if frozen

6 ounces ham steak, cut into ½-inch cubes

4 green onions, thinly sliced

2 teaspoons vegetable oil

6 ounces fresh mozzarella cheese, cut into ½-inch cubes

1 Preheat broiler.

2 Cook noodles according to package directions. Drain and rinse with cold water.

3 Whisk eggs and 1 teaspoon of the seasoning packet in large bowl. Discard remaining seasoning packet. Stir in edamame, ham, green onions and noodles.

4 Heat oil in 12-inch broiler-proof skillet over medium heat. Add egg mixture; stir gently to form large curds. Top with mozzarella cheese. Cover; cook 6 minutes or until edge of eggs are set. Run rubber spatula along side occasionally to prevent sticking.

5 Uncover skillet; transfer to broiler. Broil 6 minutes or until frittata is puffed and set. Let stand 5 minutes. Slide onto serving plate or cutting board; cut into wedges.

Makes 4 to 6 servings

7-Layer Dip

1   package (3 ounces) ramen noodles, any flavor, crushed*

2   tablespoons dried taco seasoning mix

3   ripe avocados, diced

1   jalapeño, finely chopped**

2   tablespoons finely chopped fresh cilantro

2   tablespoons lime juice

1   clove garlic, minced

½   teaspoon salt

1   can (about 15 ounces) refried beans

1   container (16 ounces) sour cream

2   cups shredded Mexican Cheddar-Jack cheese

2   medium tomatoes, diced

3   green onions, thinly sliced

    Tortilla chips

Discard seasoning packet.

**Jalapeño peppers can sting and irritate the skin. So wear rubber gloves when handling peppers and do not touch your eyes.*

1 Combine noodles with taco seasoning mix in medium bowl ; mix well.

2 Mash avocados, jalapeño, cilantro, lime juice, garlic and salt in large bowl.

3 Spread refried beans in bottom of 8-inch glass baking dish. Layer sour cream, noodles, avocado mixture, cheese, tomatoes and green onions evenly over beans. Serve immediately or cover and refrigerate for up to 8 hours. Serve with tortilla chips.

Makes 10 servings

Coconut Shrimp

Spicy Orange-Mustard Sauce (recipe follows)

¾   cup all-purpose flour

¾   cup beer or water

1   egg

¾   teaspoon baking powder

½   teaspoon salt

¼   teaspoon ground red pepper

1   cup flaked coconut

2   packages (3 ounces each) ramen noodles, any flavor, crushed*

20   jumbo raw shrimp, peeled and deveined

2   cups vegetable oil

*Discard seasoning packets.

1 Prepare Spicy Orange-Mustard Sauce.

2 Whisk flour, beer, egg, baking powder, salt and red pepper in medium bowl. Combine coconut and noodles in another medium bowl. Dip shrimp in beer batter; shake off excess. Coat with coconut mixture.

3 Heat oil in large skillet to 350°F. Cook shrimp in batches 3 minutes or just until golden, turning once halfway through cooking. Drain on paper towel-lined plate. Serve with Spicy Orange-Mustard Sauce.

Makes 4 servings

Spicy Orange-Mustard Sauce: Combine ¼ cup coarse grain or Dijon mustard, 2 tablespoons honey, 2 tablespoons orange juice, 2 teaspoons orange peel, ½ teaspoon ground red pepper and ¼ teaspoon ground ginger in small bowl until blended.

Tip:

Use one hand to dip the shrimp in the beer batter and the other hand to coat with coconut mixture. This way, your hands will not mix up the mixtures and create a larger mess.

Chicken Nuggets
with Spicy Tomato Dipping Sauce

½   cup panko bread crumbs

½   cup grated Parmesan cheese

1   package (3 ounces) ramen noodles, any flavor, finely crushed*

1   teaspoon garlic powder

1   teaspoon dried basil

½   teaspoon salt

¼   teaspoon black pepper

1   egg, lightly beaten

1½   pounds boneless skinless chicken breasts, cut into 1×2½-inch strips

½   cup vegetable oil

Discard seasoning packet.

1 Combine panko, cheese, crushed noodles, garlic powder, basil, salt and pepper in large bowl. Place egg in shallow dish. Dip chicken in egg; shake off excess. Coat with crumb mixture.

2 Heat oil in large skillet over medium heat. Cook chicken in batches about 5 minutes or until cooked through, turning once. Serve with Spicy Tomato Dipping Sauce.

Makes 4 servings

Spicy Tomato Dipping Sauce

1   tablespoon olive oil

1   small onion, chopped

2   cloves garlic, minced

¼   teaspoon ground red pepper

1   can (about 14 ounces) fire-roasted diced tomatoes

14

Simple Starters

1 Heat oil in medium skillet. Add onion and garlic; cook and stir about 3 minutes or until onion is tender and golden brown. Stir in red pepper.

2 Remove skillet from heat; add tomatoes. Process in blender or food processor until smooth. Return to skillet and cook about 10 minutes or until thickened and reduced to 1½ cups.

Makes 1½ cups dip

Crispy Ramen Noodle Pancake

  2   packages (3 ounces each) chicken-flavored ramen noodles*

  2   green onions, thinly sliced

  2   tablespoons water

  2   teaspoons oyster sauce

  1   teaspoon cornstarch

 ⅛   teaspoon black pepper

  3   tablespoons vegetable oil, divided

  3   ounces shiitake mushrooms, stems removed, sliced

  2   medium heads bok choy, cut into ¼-inch-wide strips

Reserve one seasoning packet, discard the other seasoning packet.

1 Cook noodles according to package directions. Drain and rinse with cold water. Transfer to large bowl. Toss with green onions and 1 seasoning packet; discard remaining seasoning packet.

2 Combine water, oyster sauce, cornstarch and pepper in small bowl.

3 Heat 1 tablespoon oil in large skillet over medium-high heat. Add noodle mixture to skillet; press down evenly with spatula to form a pancake. Cook 5 to 7 minutes or until bottom is crisp and golden brown. Slide onto serving plate; add 1 tablespoon oil to skillet. Invert pancake into skillet and cook 5 minutes until crisp and golden brown. Return pancake to plate and keep warm.

4 Heat remaining 1 tablespoon oil in skillet. Add mushrooms; cook 2 minutes or until tender, stirring occasionally. Add bok choy; cook 2 minutes or until stems are crisp-tender. Add sauce mixture and cook 30 seconds or until vegetables are glazed, stirring frequently. Spoon vegetables over pancake.

Makes 1 large (8-inch) pancake or 2 servings

Simple Starters

Mediterranean Chickpea Ramen Salad

   2   **packages (3 ounces each) ramen noodles, any flavor, broken into small pieces***

        Juice of 1 lemon

   3   **tablespoons extra virgin olive oil**

   1   **teaspoon kosher salt**

 ½   **teaspoon black pepper**

   1   **can (about 15 ounces) chickpeas, rinsed and drained**

   2   **tomatoes, diced**

 ¾   **cup crumbled feta cheese**

 ½   **cup diced red onion**

 ½   **English cucumber, seeded and diced**

 ¼   **cup finely chopped Italian parsley**

*Discard seasoning packets.

1 Cook noodles according to package directions; drain well.

2 Whisk lemon juice, oil, salt and pepper in large bowl. Add chickpeas, tomatoes, feta cheese, onion, cucumber, parsley and noodles; toss to combine.

Makes 6 to 8 servings

Mushroom Pilaf

　2　tablespoons butter, divided

　1　package (3 ounces) oriental ramen noodles, crumbled

½　cup chopped pecans

　1　package (8 ounces) sliced mushrooms

　2　cups hot cooked rice

　2　tablespoons chopped fresh parsley

1 Melt 1 tablespoon butter in large skillet over medium-high heat. Add noodles and pecans; cook and stir 3 minutes or until toasted. Remove to plate.

2 Melt remaining 1 tablespoon butter in skillet. Add mushrooms; cook and stir 8 minutes or until browned.

3 Reduce heat to medium; add rice, seasoning packet from noodles, noodle mixture and parsley; cook and stir 2 minutes or until heated through.

Makes 4 servings

Tips:

If this dish will not be served right away, reserve the toasted noodles and pecans. Fold into pilaf just before serving so they stay crisp.

Add 1½ cups chopped cooked chicken to this pilaf to make a main dish.

Broccoli Slaw

1	package (12 ounces) broccoli slaw
6	slices bacon, crisp-cooked and crumbled
½	small red onion, chopped
1	package (3 ounces) ramen noodles, any flavor, broken into small pieces, divided*
¼	cup roasted salted sunflower seeds
1	cup reduced-fat mayonnaise
2	tablespoons sugar
2	tablespoons cider vinegar
¼	teaspoon black pepper

*Discard seasoning packet.

1 Combine broccoli slaw, bacon, onion, half of noodles and sunflower seeds in large bowl.

2 Whisk mayonnaise, sugar, vinegar and pepper in small bowl. Pour over slaw mixture; stir to combine. Garnish with remaining noodles. Serve immediately.

Makes 6 to 8 servings

Tip:

Any chopped nuts, such as peanuts or almonds, can be substituted for the sunflower seeds.

Creamy Noodle Kugel

3   **packages (3 ounces each) ramen noodles, any flavor***

¾   **cup cottage cheese**

¾   **cup sour cream**

2   **eggs**

⅓   **cup granulated sugar**

½   **cup golden raisins (optional)**

2   **tablespoons packed brown sugar**

*Discard seasoning packets.

1 Preheat oven to 350°F. Spray 9-inch glass baking dish with nonstick cooking spray.

2 Bring water to a boil in large saucepan. Boil noodles 2 minutes. Drain and rinse with cold water.

3 Whisk cottage cheese, sour cream, eggs and granulated sugar in large bowl. Add noodles and raisins, if desired; toss to coat. Pour into prepared dish. Sprinkle with brown sugar.

4 Bake 35 to 40 minutes or until center is set. Serve warm or at room temperature.

Makes 8 servings

Green Bean Mushroom Casserole

1	pound fresh green beans, ends trimmed
4	tablespoons vegetable oil, divided
4	shallots, thinly sliced
8	ounces cremini mushrooms, quartered
1	can (10¾ ounces) condensed cream of mushroom soup
½	cup milk
¼	teaspoon freshly ground black pepper
⅛	teaspoon salt
1	package (3 ounces) ramen noodles, any flavor, broken into small pieces*

Discard seasoning packet.

1 Preheat oven to 350°F. Bring water to a boil in large saucepan over high heat. Add green beans and cook 4 minutes. Drain and rinse with cold water.

2 Heat 3 tablespoons oil in large skillet over medium heat. Add shallots; cook 10 minutes or until softened and golden brown. Drain on paper towels. Heat remaining 1 tablespoon oil in skillet over medium-high heat. Add mushrooms; cook 7 minutes or until browned.

3 Combine soup, milk and pepper in large bowl. Add beans and mushrooms. Spoon into ungreased 1½-quart casserole; bake 20 minutes. Increase oven temperature to 400°F. Combine shallots, salt and noodles; sprinkle over casserole. Bake 5 minutes.

Makes 6 servings

Noodlicious Salads & Sides

Greek Noodle Salad

2   packages (3 ounces each) ramen noodles, any flavor, broken in half*

3   tablespoons olive oil

Juice of 1 lemon

2   tablespoons red wine vinegar

1   teaspoon dried oregano

1   tomato, chopped

¾   cup diced cucumber

½   cup crumbled feta cheese

¼   cup chopped kalamata olives

Discard seasoning packets.

1 Bring water to a boil in medium saucepan. Boil noodles 2 minutes. Drain and rinse with cold water.

2 Combine oil, lemon juice, vinegar and oregano in large bowl. Add noodles, tomato, cucumber, cheese and olives; toss to coat.

Makes 4 to 6 servings

 Tip:

This easy-to-prepare salad makes a delicious side for baked or grilled fish.

Tuna Ramen Noodle Salad

½ package (3 ounces) Oriental-flavor ramen noodle soup mix

1 (2.6-ounce) STARKIST Flavor Fresh Pouch® Tuna (Albacore or Chunk Light)

½ cup julienne-strip cucumber

½ cup julienne-strip green or red bell pepper

½ cup sliced water chestnuts, cut into halves

Dressing

2 tablespoons rice or white vinegar

2 teaspoons sesame oil

1 teaspoon peanut butter

⅛ teaspoon crushed red pepper

Cook ramen noodles according to package directions. Drain broth, reserving if desired to use as a clear soup for another meal. In a medium bowl toss noodles with tuna, cucumber, bell pepper and water chestnuts.

For Dressing, in a small shaker jar combine vinegar, oil, peanut butter and crushed red pepper. Cover and shake until well blended. Toss with noodle mixture. Serve immediately.

Makes 1 serving

Southwestern Salad

2 hearts of Romaine lettuce, cut crosswise into ½-inch-thick strips

1 cup frozen corn, thawed

1 cup halved cherry tomatoes

8 ounces cooked boneless skinless chicken breast, diced

1 ripe avocado, diced

1 red bell pepper, diced

1 can (about 15 ounces) black beans, rinsed and drained

Dressing

1½ tablespoons minced shallot

¼ cup lime juice

2 teaspoons honey

⅓ cup olive oil

½ teaspoon kosher salt

¼ teaspoon black pepper

2 tablespoons finely chopped fresh cilantro (optional)

1 package (3 ounces) ramen noodles, any flavor, broken into small pieces*

Discard seasoning packet.

1 Combine Romaine, corn, tomatoes, chicken, avocado, bell pepper and black beans in large bowl; toss well.

2 Whisk shallot, lime juice, honey, oil, salt, black pepper and cilantro in medium bowl. Add to salad mixture; toss to coat. Sprinkle with noodles.

Makes 4 to 6 servings

Noodlicious Salads & Sides

Thai Beef Salad
with Cucumber Dressing

Cucumber Dressing (recipe follows)

1 pound extra-lean (90% lean) ground beef

½ red bell pepper, cut into thin strips

6 mushrooms, quartered

2 green onions, diagonally cut into 1-inch pieces

1 clove garlic, minced

1 tablespoon seasoned rice vinegar

1 teaspoon soy sauce

1 package (3 ounces) beef-flavored ramen noodles

Lettuce leaves

12 cherry tomatoes, halved (optional)

Mint sprigs (optional)

1 Prepare Cucumber Dressing; set aside. Brown beef in medium skillet. Drain. Add red bell pepper, mushrooms, green onions and garlic; cook until tender. Stir in vinegar, soy sauce and seasoning packet from ramen noodles.

2 Cook noodles according to package directions. Drain. Cool in bowl of ice water. Drain well before serving.

3 Arrange lettuce on four plates. Top with noodles and beef mixture. Garnish with tomatoes and mint. Serve with the dressing.

Makes 4 servings

Noodlicious Salads & Sides

Cucumber Dressing

1   medium cucumber, coarsely chopped

½   cup coarsely chopped onion

½   cup loosely packed cilantro leaves

1   clove garlic, minced

1   tablespoon diced jalapeño or green chile pepper*

½   cup seasoned rice vinegar

*Jalapeño and chili peppers can sting and irritate the skin, so wear rubber gloves when handling peppers and do not touch your eyes.

Place cucumber, onion, cilantro, garlic and jalapeño in food processor container; process 1 minute. Spoon mixture into small bowl; stir in vinegar.

Creamy and Crunchy Coleslaw

1	tablespoon vegetable oil
2	packages (3 ounces) ramen noodles, any flavor*
½	cup sliced almonds
½	cup mayonnaise
¼	cup rice wine vinegar
2	teaspoons honey
1	teaspoon sesame oil
1	teaspoon soy sauce
	Hot sauce, to taste
2	cups shredded Napa cabbage
½	cup sliced green onions

*Discard seasoning packets.

1 Heat vegetable oil in medium skillet over medium heat. Crush half of one package noodles into skillet; cook and stir 2 minutes. Add almonds; cook and stir 2 minutes or until golden brown. Transfer to plate.

2 Bring water to a boil in medium saucepan over medium-high heat. Add remaining noodles; cook 2 minutes. Drain and rinse with cold water.

3 Combine mayonnaise, vinegar, honey, sesame oil, soy sauce and hot sauce in large bowl; mix well. Add boiled noodles, cabbage and green onions; toss to coat. Top with toasted noodles and almonds just before serving.

Makes 6 servings

Asian Shrimp & Noodle Salad

⅓   cup plus 2 tablespoons vegetable oil, divided

¼   cup cider vinegar

2   tablespoons FRENCH'S® Worcestershire Sauce

2   tablespoons light soy sauce

2   tablespoons honey

1   teaspoon grated fresh ginger or ¼ teaspoon ground ginger

2   packages (3 ounces each) chicken-flavor ramen noodle soup

1   pound shrimp, cleaned and deveined with tails left on

2   cups vegetables such as broccoli, carrots and snow peas, cut into bite-size pieces

1⅓   cups FRENCH'S® French Fried Onions, divided

1 Combine ⅓ cup oil, vinegar, Worcestershire, soy sauce, honey and ginger until well blended; set aside. Prepare ramen noodles according to package directions for soup; drain and rinse noodles. Place in large serving bowl.

2 Stir-fry shrimp in 1 tablespoon oil in large skillet over medium-high heat, stirring constantly, until shrimp turn pink. Remove shrimp to bowl with noodles. Stir-fry vegetables in remaining oil in skillet over medium-high heat, stirring constantly, until vegetables are crisp-tender.

3 Add vegetable mixture, dressing and 1 cup French Fried Onions to bowl with noodles; toss to coat well. Serve immediately topped with remaining ⅓ cup onions.

Makes 6 servings

Sunflower Salad

1	package beef ramen noodles, broken into pieces
3	cups shredded cabbage
⅓	cup chopped onion
1	large tomato, chopped
2	tablespoons bacon bits
¼	cup sunflower kernels, roasted, no salt
¼	cup shredded cheddar cheese

Boil ramen noodles for 3 to 4 minutes. Drain and rinse with cold water. Refrigerate until cool. Combine all salad ingredients in a large bowl and prepare dressing.

Dressing

¼	cup sugar
3	tablespoons sunflower oil
1½	tablespoons vinegar
1	beef seasoning packet from ramen noodles

Mix ingredients together and add to salad. Refrigerate before serving.

Makes 4 to 5 main dish servings

Favorite recipe from **National Sunflower Association**

Mandarin Salad

⅓ cup olive oil

2 tablespoons cider vinegar

2 teaspoons honey

2 teaspoons dried tarragon

½ teaspoon dry mustard

¼ teaspoon salt

⅛ teaspoon ground black pepper

1 can (11 ounces) mandarin oranges, drained, and 1 tablespoon juice reserved

4 cups chopped Romaine lettuce

1 package (3 ounces) ramen noodles, any flavor, lightly crushed*

½ cup toasted pecans, coarsely chopped**

¼ cup chopped red onion

*Discard seasoning packet.

**To toast pecans. Spread in single layer in small heavy skillet. Cook over medium heat 1 to 2 minutes or until nuts are lightly browned, stirring frequently. Remove from skillet immediately. Cool before using.

1 Whisk oil, vinegar, honey, tarragon, mustard, salt, pepper and reserved mandarin orange juice in large bowl.

2 Add lettuce, oranges, noodles, pecans and onion to dressing; toss to combine.

Makes 4 servings

Cheesy Italian Noodle Bake

4   packages (3 ounces each) ramen noodles, any flavor*

1   pound sweet Italian sausage, casings removed

2   teaspoons olive oil

1   cup diced onion

1   cup diced red bell pepper

1   teaspoon minced garlic

1   can (about 15 ounces) tomato sauce

½   cup thinly sliced fresh basil

2   cups shredded mozzarella cheese

Discard seasoning packets.

1 Preheat oven to 400°F. Grease 13×9-inch baking dish.

2 Cook noodles according to package directions. Drain and rinse with cold water. Transfer to large bowl.

3 Brown sausage in large skillet over medium-high heat 8 minutes or until well browned, stirring to break up meat. Drain on paper towel-lined plate. Transfer to bowl with noodles.

4 Heat oil in skillet. Add onion and bell pepper; cook and stir 6 minutes or until softened. Add garlic; cook 30 seconds. Combine with noodle mixture. Add tomato sauce and basil; stir until combined.

5 Spread mixture evenly in prepared dish. Sprinkle with cheese. Bake 25 to 30 minutes or until bubbly and cheese is golden brown. Let stand 5 minutes before serving.

Makes 8 to 10 servings

Swedish "Meatball" Burgers

  3   **tablespoons butter, divided**

  1   **small onion, chopped**

¼   **cup milk**

  2   **packages (3 ounces each) ramen noodles, any flavor, crushed***

  1   **egg**

  1   **teaspoon salt, divided**

½   **teaspoon black pepper, divided**

¼   **teaspoon ground allspice**

1½ **pounds ground beef**

¼   **cup all-purpose flour**

  1   **can (about 14 ounces) beef broth**

½   **cup whipping cream**

     Hard rolls (optional)

     Cranberry sauce (optional)

*Discard seasoning packets.

1 Melt 2 tablespoons butter in medium saucepan over medium heat. Add onion; cook 3 minutes or until translucent. Reduce heat to medium-low; add milk. Bring to a simmer. Add crushed noodles; remove from heat.

2 Whisk egg, ½ teaspoon salt, ¼ teaspoon pepper and allspice in large bowl. Add noodle mixture; stir to combine. Add beef; stir until well blended. Shape into 6 patties.

3 Preheat broiler. Broil burgers on rack 4 inches from heat 10 minutes until medium-rare (145°F), or desired doneness.

4 Melt remaining 1 tablespoon butter in saucepan. Add flour; cook 2 to 3 minutes or until lightly browned, whisking constantly. Gradually whisk in broth and cream. Bring to a boil; cook 2 minutes or until thickened. Stir in remaining salt and pepper.

5 Serve burgers on rolls with cream sauce and cranberry sauce, if desired.

Makes 6 servings

Dinner Winners

Chicken Parmesan

½ cup all-purpose flour

1 egg, lightly beaten

1 package (3 ounces) ramen noodles, any flavor*

½ cup Parmesan cheese

1 teaspoon dried basil

½ teaspoon dried rosemary

½ cup shredded Italian cheese blend

4 boneless skinless chicken breasts (about 1 pound)

2 tablespoons olive oil

1 cup pasta sauce, plus additional for dipping

Discard seasoning packet.

1 Preheat oven to 350°F.

2 Place flour in shallow dish. Place egg in shallow bowl. Place noodles, Parmesan cheese, basil and rosemary in food processor; process until fine crumbs are formed. Reserve ¼ cup mixture. Place remaining mixture in another shallow dish. Combine reserved noodle mixture with Italian cheese blend in medium bowl.

3 Dip chicken into flour, then egg, then noodle mixture. Place on clean plate.

4 Heat oil in large ovenproof skillet. Cook chicken 8 minutes per side or until golden brown. Top with sauce and cheese mixture. Bake 15 minutes or until no longer pink in center. Serve with additional sauce.

Makes 4 servings

Denver Quiche

1   package (3 ounces) chicken-flavored ramen noodles*

1   tablespoon vegetable oil

½   cup diced red or green bell pepper

¼   cup diced yellow onion

½   cup diced ham

6   eggs

1   cup fat-free milk

½   cup Cheddar cheese, shredded

     Salt and black pepper

Discard seasoning packet.

1 Preheat oven to 375°F. Spray 9-inch pie plate with nonstick cooking spray.

2 Cook noodles according to package directions. Drain and rinse with cold water. Press noodles onto bottom of pie plate; bake 10 minutes or until lightly browned. Cool completely.

3 Heat oil in medium skillet. Add bell pepper and onion and cook 3 minutes or until crisp-tender. Add ham; cook until heated through. Spoon into crust.

4 Beat eggs and milk in medium bowl until blended. Add cheese, salt and black pepper; mix well. Carefully pour over ham mixture.

5 Bake 35 minutes or until center is puffed and knife inserted near center comes out clean. Let stand 5 minutes. Cut into wedges.

Makes 6 servings

Cheesy Hamburger Ramen

1	pound ground beef
1	cup diced red onion
1	teaspoon salt, divided
2	packages (3 ounces each) ramen noodles, any flavor*
1	tablespoon unsalted butter
1	tablespoon all-purpose flour
1¼	cups milk
¼	teaspoon black pepper
1	can (about 14 ounces) diced tomatoes, drained
1½	cups shredded sharp Cheddar cheese
¼	cup ketchup

Discard seasoning packets.

1 Heat large nonstick skillet over medium-high heat. Add beef; cook 2 minutes or just until beginning to brown. Add onion and ½ teaspoon salt; cook 8 minutes or until onion is softened. Transfer to large bowl; cover to keep warm.

2 Cook noodles according to package directions; drain well. Transfer to large bowl.

3 Add butter to skillet; melt over medium heat. Stir in flour; cook 1 minute. Slowly add milk, stirring constantly. Add pepper and remaining ½ teaspoon salt; cook 4 minutes or until mixture is thickened, stirring constantly. Remove from heat. Add tomatoes, cheese and ketchup; stir until cheese is melted. Add sauce to bowl; stir to combine. Serve immediately.

Makes 4 servings

Scallop Stir-Fry

2   packages (3 ounces each) ramen noodles, any flavor*

1   tablespoon olive oil

1   pound asparagus, cut into 1-inch pieces

1   red bell pepper, cut into thin rings

3   green onions, chopped

1   clove garlic, minced

1   pound sea scallops, halved crosswise

2   tablespoons soy sauce

1   teaspoon hot pepper sauce

1   teaspoon sesame oil

     Juice of ½ lime

Discard seasoning packets.

1 Cook noodles in lightly salted boiling water according to package directions.

2 Meanwhile, heat olive oil in wok or large skillet over high heat. Add asparagus, bell pepper, green onions and garlic; stir-fry 2 minutes. Add scallops; stir-fry until scallops turn opaque.

3 Stir in soy sauce, hot pepper sauce, sesame oil and lime juice. Add noodles; heat through, stirring occasionally.

Makes 4 servings

Lemon Herbed Tilapia

2   tablespoons melted butter

     Grated peel and juice of 1 lemon, divided

1   package (3 ounces) ramen noodles, any flavor*

1   teaspoon dried dill weed

1   teaspoon dried basil

1   teaspoon dried parsley

4   tilapia fillets (about 4 ounces each)

Discard seasoning packet.

1 Preheat oven to 425°F. Line baking sheet with parchment paper.

2 Combine melted butter and lemon juice in shallow bowl. Combine noodles, dill, basil, parsley and lemon peel in food processor or blender. Process until fine crumbs are formed; pour onto plate.

3 Dip tilapia into butter mixture, then press into noodle mixture. Place on prepared baking sheet.

4 Bake 12 minutes or until fish flakes when tested with fork.

Makes 4 servings

Dinner Winners

Ramen Chili

2   teaspoons vegetable oil

2   pounds ground beef

2   red onions, diced

1   red bell pepper, diced

6   tablespoons chili powder

4   teaspoons salt

2   teaspoons ground cumin

¼   teaspoon ground red pepper

4   cans (about 14 ounces each) diced tomatoes with basil, garlic and oregano

2   cans (about 15 ounces each) kidney beans, rinsed and drained

2   cups water

1   package (3 ounces) ramen noodles, any flavor, broken*

1   tablespoon light brown sugar

Sour cream, shredded Cheddar cheese and thinly sliced green onions (optional)

Discard seasoning packet.

1 Heat oil in Dutch oven over medium-high heat. Add beef; brown 6 to 8 minutes, stirring to break up meat. Transfer to large bowl with slotted spoon. Add onions and bell pepper to Dutch oven; cook 6 minutes or until softened. Add chili powder, salt, cumin and ground red pepper; cook and stir 1 minute.

2 Return beef to Dutch oven; stir in tomatoes, beans, water, noodles and brown sugar. Bring to a boil; reduce heat to medium-low and simmer 45 minutes to 1 hour, stirring occasionally. Top with sour cream, cheese and green onions, if desired.

Makes 8 to 10 servings

Stuffed Bell Peppers

3	large red bell peppers, halved lengthwise and seeded
1	package (3 ounces) ramen noodles, any flavor, cut into fourths*
6	slices bacon, diced
1	cup finely chopped onion
1	teaspoon minced garlic
¼	teaspoon black pepper
1	can (about 15 ounces) cannellini beans, rinsed and drained
¾	cup shredded Gruyère cheese
1	tablespoon plus 1½ teaspoons finely chopped fresh parsley

*Discard seasoning packet.

1 Preheat oven to 400°F. Place bell peppers, cut sides up, in 13×9-inch baking pan.

2 Cook noodles in boiling water in large saucepan over medium heat 2 minutes. Drain and rinse with cold water until cool. Transfer to large bowl.

3 Heat large nonstick skillet over medium-high heat. Add bacon; cook 6 to 7 minutes or until crisp and browned. Transfer to paper towel-lined plate with slotted spoon. Drain and discard all but 2 teaspoons drippings from skillet. Add onion to skillet; cook 5 minutes or until softened. Add garlic and black pepper; cook and stir 30 seconds. Transfer to bowl with noodles; stir in beans, cheese, and bacon.

4 Stuff bean mixture evenly inside bell peppers. Bake 30 minutes or until filling is heated through and bell peppers are softened. Sprinkle evenly with parsley.

Makes 6 servings

Eggplant Parmesan

       2   eggs
       1   teaspoon dried basil
      ½   teaspoon salt
      ¼   teaspoon black pepper
      ½   cup plus 2 tablespoons grated Parmesan cheese, divided
       1   package (3 ounces) ramen noodles, any flavor, crushed*
      ¼   cup panko or other bread crumbs
       2   medium eggplants (1 pound each), cut lengthwise into ¾-inch slices
       2   cups vegetable oil
       1   cup low-fat ricotta cheese
       8   ounces shredded mozzarella cheese
       1   jar (about 28 ounces) tomato sauce

Discard seasoning packet.

1 Preheat oven to 350°F. Spray a 9×13-inch baking pan with cooking spray.

2 Beat eggs, basil, salt and pepper in shallow dish until blended. Combine ½ cup Parmesan cheese, crushed noodles and bread crumbs in another shallow dish. Dip eggplant in egg mixture; shake off excess. Coat both sides with crumb mixture.

3 Heat oil in large skillet. Cook eggplant in batches 4 minutes or until golden, turning once. Drain on paper towel-lined plate.

4 Combine ricotta cheese and mozzarella cheese in small bowl. Place one-third of eggplant in bottom of prepared pan. Spread about 1 cup tomato sauce over eggplant. Top with half of cheese mixture; repeat layers ending with sauce. Bake 30 minutes or until eggplant is fork-tender and cheese is melted.

5 Preheat broiler. Sprinkle remaining 2 tablespoons Parmesan cheese over eggplant. Broil 6 inches from heat 3 minutes or until cheese is browned. Let stand 10 minutes before serving.

Makes 12 servings

Teriyaki Meatloaf

1	tablespoon vegetable oil
1	package (8 ounces) thinly sliced mushrooms
½	cup chopped green onions
1	package (3 ounces) ramen noodles, any flavor, crushed*
½	cup teriyaki sauce
1	egg, lightly beaten
1½	pounds (24 ounces) ground beef

Discard seasoning packet.

1 Preheat oven to 375°F.

2 Heat oil in medium skillet over medium-high heat. Add mushrooms; cook and stir 10 minutes. Add green onions; cook and stir 1 minute. Transfer to large bowl. Add crushed noodles, teriyaki sauce and egg; stir well. Fold in beef.

3 Press beef mixture into 8×4-inch loaf pan. Bake 35 to 40 minutes or until cooked through (160°F). Let stand 10 minutes before slicing.

Makes 4 to 6 servings

Tip:

Serve leftovers on toasted bread or rolls as a meatloaf sandwich. A great brown bag lunch idea!

Easy Asian Chicken Skillet

2	packages (3 ounces each) chicken-flavored ramen noodles
1	package (10 ounces) frozen broccoli florets, thawed
1	package (9 ounces) frozen baby carrots, thawed
1	tablespoon vegetable oil
1	pound boneless skinless chicken breasts, cut into thin strips
1	can (8 ounces) sliced water chestnuts, drained
¼	cup stir-fry sauce

1 Remove seasoning packets from noodles. Save one packet for another use.

2 Bring 4 cups water to a boil in large saucepan. Add noodles, broccoli and carrots. Cook over medium-high heat 5 minutes, stirring occasionally; drain.

3 Heat oil in large nonstick skillet over medium-high heat. Add chicken; cook and stir about 8 minutes or until browned.

4 Stir in noodle mixture, water chestnuts, stir-fry sauce and one seasoning packet; cook until heated through.

Makes 4 to 6 servings

Dinner Winners

Curried Turkey Noodle Soup

   1   tablespoon olive oil

   ¾   pound turkey breast tenderloin, cut into bite-size pieces

   5   cups water

   2   packages (3 ounces each) chicken-flavored ramen noodles

   1   tablespoon curry powder

   ⅛   teaspoon salt

   1   cup sliced celery

   1   medium apple, cored and chopped (1½ cups)

   ¼   cup dry roasted unsalted peanuts

1 Heat oil in large saucepan over medium-high heat. Add turkey; cook and stir 3 to 4 minutes or until no longer pink. Remove turkey; set aside.

2 Add water, seasoning packets from noodles, curry powder and salt to saucepan. Bring to a boil. Reduce heat; cover and simmer 5 minutes.

3 Break up noodles; gently stir noodles and celery into saucepan. Bring mixture to a boil. Reduce heat and simmer, uncovered, 5 minutes.

4 Stir in turkey and apple. Cook until heated through. Ladle into soup bowls. Sprinkle with peanuts.

Makes 5 servings

French Onion Soup

4 tablespoons butter

1 package (3 ounces) ramen noodles, any flavor, broken into small pieces*

4 sweet yellow onions (about 2 pounds), thinly sliced

2 teaspoons sugar

1 teaspoon all-purpose flour

½ teaspoon salt

¼ teaspoon black pepper

1 cup white wine

2 cans (about 14 ounces each) reduced-sodium beef broth

1 8-inch loaf French bread, sliced into 8 rounds

1 cup (about 4 ounces) shredded fontina cheese

*Discard seasoning packet.

1 Melt butter in large saucepan over medium heat. Add noodles; cook and stir 2 to 3 minutes or until golden. Add onions; cook 20 to 25 minutes or until golden and translucent, stirring occasionally.

2 Combine sugar, flour, salt and pepper; add to noodle mixture. Add wine. Cook 3 minutes or until wine evaporates, stirring to scrape up browned bits. Add broth; bring to a boil. Reduce heat and simmer, partially covered, 10 minutes.

3 Preheat oven to 450°F. Line baking sheet with foil. Toast bread slices 5 minutes or until lightly browned. Sprinkle toast evenly with cheese; bake 3 minutes or until melted. Divide soup into bowls; top each with 2 slices toast. Serve immediately.

Makes 4 servings

Tip:

If you have four individual heatproof bowls, the toast can be baked directly on top of the soup.

Shortcut Chicken Tortilla Soup

2　cans (about 14 ounces each) reduced-sodium chicken broth

4　boneless skinless chicken breasts (about 1 pound)

2　jars (16 ounces each) corn and black bean salsa

3　tablespoons vegetable oil

1　tablespoon taco seasoning

1　package (3 ounces) ramen noodles, any flavor, broken into small pieces*

4　ounces Monterey Jack cheese, grated

*Discard seasoning packet.

1 Bring broth to a simmer in large saucepan. Add chicken; cook 12 to 15 minutes or until no longer pink in center. Remove chicken from saucepan; set aside until cool enough to handle. Shred chicken with two forks.

2 Add salsa to saucepan; cook 5 minutes or until soup comes to a simmer. Return shredded chicken to saucepan; cook 5 minutes more until thoroughly heated through.

3 Combine oil and taco seasoning in small bowl. Add noodles; toss to coat. Cook and stir noodles in medium skillet over medium heat 8 to 10 minutes or until toasted. Top soup with toasted noodles and grated cheese.

Makes 6 servings

Tip:

Serve soup with lime wedges, chopped avocado or fresh cilantro on the side—top with your favorites.

Asian Noodle Soup

1½   cups water

1   Asian Noodle Soup Mix (recipe follows)

½   cup fresh or frozen snow peas or sugar snap peas

1 Heat water in small saucepan over high heat until boiling. Add soup mix and peas; stir until blended.

2 Reduce heat to medium; simmer 3 minutes or until noodles are tender.

Makes 1 serving

Asian Noodle Soup Mix

½   of a 3-ounce package ramen noodles, any flavor, including half of seasoning packet

1   teaspoon dried chives

¼   teaspoon sesame seeds

¼   teaspoon granulated garlic

⅛   teaspoon ground ginger

1   individually wrapped fortune cookie

1 Break noodles into chunks and place in small bowl. Sprinkle ½ of noodle seasoning packet, chives, sesame seeds, garlic and ginger over noodles. (Save remaining noodles and seasoning for another use.) Spoon mixture into small food storage bag. Seal; place in mug. Place wrapped fortune cookie in mug.

2 Decorate mug and attach gift tag with preparation instructions.

Makes 1 soup mix

Apricot Beef with Sesame Noodles

1   beef top sirloin steak (about 1 pound)

3   tablespoons Dijon mustard

3   tablespoons soy sauce

2   packages (3 ounces each) ramen noodles

2   tablespoons vegetable oil

2   cups (6 ounces) snow peas

1   medium red bell pepper, cut into cubes

¾   cup apricot preserves

½   cup beef broth

3   tablespoons chopped green onions

2   tablespoons toasted sesame seeds*, divided

To toast sesame seeds, spread in a dry, heavy skillet over medium heat 2 minutes or until golden, stirring frequently.

1 Cut beef lengthwise in half, then crosswise into ¼-inch strips. Combine beef, mustard and soy sauce in medium resealable food storage bag. Seal bag. Shake to evenly distribute marinade; refrigerate 4 hours or overnight.

2 Cook noodles according to package directions, discarding seasoning packets.

3 Heat oil in large skillet over medium-high heat until hot. Add half of beef with marinade; stir-fry 2 minutes. Remove to bowl. Repeat with remaining beef and marinade. Return beef to skillet. Add snow peas and bell pepper; stir-fry 2 minutes. Add noodles, preserves, broth, green onions and 1 tablespoon sesame seeds. Cook 1 minute or until heated through. Top with remaining sesame seeds before serving.

Makes 4 to 6 servings

Noodle Bowls

Asian Chicken Noodle Soup

3½   cups Swanson® Chicken Broth (Regular, Natural Goodness® **or** Certified Organic)

1   teaspoon soy sauce

1   teaspoon ground ginger

Generous dash ground black pepper

1   medium carrot, diagonally sliced

1   stalk celery, diagonally sliced

½   red pepper, cut into 2-inch-long strips

2   green onions, diagonally sliced

1   clove garlic, minced

½   cup broken-up **uncooked** curly Asian noodles

1   cup shredded cooked chicken

1 Heat the broth, soy sauce, ginger, black pepper, carrot, celery, red pepper, green onions and garlic in a 2-quart saucepan over medium-high heat to a boil.

2 Stir the noodles and chicken in the saucepan. Reduce the heat to medium and cook for 10 minutes or until the noodles are done.

Makes 4 servings

Prep Time: 5 minutes
Cook Time: 20 minutes

Tip:

For an Interesting Twist: Use **1 cup** sliced bok choy for the celery and **2 ounces uncooked** cellophane noodles for the curly Asian noodles. Reduce the cook time to 5 minutes.

Noodle Bowls

Szechuan Vegetable Lo Mein

2 cans (about 14 ounces each) vegetable broth

2 teaspoons minced garlic

1 teaspoon minced fresh ginger

¼ teaspoon red pepper flakes

1 package (16 ounces) frozen vegetable medley, such as broccoli, carrots, water chestnuts and red bell peppers

2 packages (3 ounces each) ramen noodles* or 6 ounces uncooked angel hair pasta, broken in half

3 tablespoons soy sauce

1 tablespoon dark sesame oil

¼ cup thinly sliced green onions

Discard seasoning packet.

1 Combine broth, garlic, ginger and red pepper flakes in large deep skillet. Cover and bring to a boil over high heat.

2 Add vegetables and noodles to skillet; cover and return to a boil. Reduce heat to medium-low; simmer, uncovered, 5 to 6 minutes or until vegetables and noodles are tender, stirring occasionally.

3 Stir in soy sauce and sesame oil; cook 3 minutes. Stir in green onions; ladle into bowls.

Makes 4 servings

Tip:

For a heartier, protein-packed main dish, add 1 package drained (about 14 ounces) extra firm tofu, cut into ¾-inch pieces, to the broth mixture with the soy sauce and sesame oil.

Asian Chicken Squiggle Soup

2	cups water
1	can (about 14 ounces) low-sodium chicken broth
1	cup sliced carrots
½	cup sliced green onions
½	teaspoon ground ginger
3	packages (3 ounces each) chicken-flavored ramen noodles
2	cups boneless skinless chicken breast, cooked and cut into 1-inch pieces
1	cup frozen sugar snap peas
2	tablespoons lemon juice

1 Heat water, broth, carrots, green onions and ginger in large saucepan over medium heat. Stir in contents of 1 seasoning packet from noodles; bring to a boil. (Discard remaining seasoning packets or reserve for another use.)

2 Break noodles in half; stir into vegetable mixture. Boil 2 minutes. Stir in chicken, snap peas and lemon juice; cook until heated through.

Makes 6 to 7 servings

Noodle Bowls

Asian Ramen Noodle Soup

2	cans (about 14 ounces each) chicken broth
4	ounces boneless pork loin, cut into thin strips
¾	cup thinly sliced mushrooms
½	cup firm tofu, cut into ¼-inch cubes (optional)
3	tablespoons white vinegar
3	tablespoons sherry
1	tablespoon reduced-sodium soy sauce
½	teaspoon ground red pepper
1	package (3 ounces) ramen noodles, any flavor, broken*
1	egg, beaten
¼	cup finely chopped green onions, green tops only

*Discard seasoning packet.

1 Bring broth to a boil in large saucepan over high heat; add pork, mushrooms and tofu, if desired. Reduce heat to medium-low; simmer, covered, 5 minutes. Stir in vinegar, sherry, soy sauce and red pepper.

2 Return broth mixture to a boil over high heat; stir in ramen noodles. Cook, stirring occasionally, 5 to 7 minutes or until noodles are tender. Slowly stir in egg and green onions; remove from heat. Ladle soup into individual bowls.

Makes 4 servings

Thai Noodle Soup

1	package (3 ounces) ramen noodles, any flavor
¾	pound chicken tenders
2	cans (about 14 ounces each) chicken broth
¼	cup shredded carrots
¼	cup frozen snow peas
2	tablespoons thinly sliced green onions
½	teaspoon minced garlic
¼	teaspoon ground ginger
3	tablespoons chopped fresh cilantro
½	lime, cut into 4 wedges

1 Break noodles into pieces. Cook noodles according to package directions; discard seasoning packet. Drain; set aside.

2 Cut chicken into ½-inch pieces. Combine broth and chicken in large saucepan or Dutch oven; bring to a boil over medium heat. Cook 2 minutes.

3 Add carrots, snow peas, green onions, garlic and ginger. Reduce heat to low; simmer 3 minutes. Add cooked noodles and cilantro; heat through. Serve soup with lime wedges.

Makes 4 servings

Skillet "Spaghetti" Toss

- 2   tablespoons olive oil
- 1   cup sliced mushrooms
- 1   cup broccoli florets
- 2   Italian chicken sausages, sliced
- 2   packages (3 ounces each) ramen noodles, any flavor, broken in half*
- 1   to 1½ cups pasta sauce
     Grated Parmesan cheese

*Discard seasoning packets.

1 Heat oil in large skillet over medium-high heat. Add mushrooms, broccoli and sausage; cook and stir 10 minutes or until broccoli is crisp-tender.

2 Meanwhile, bring water to a boil in medium saucepan. Boil noodles 2 minutes; drain well.

3 Add sauce and noodles to skillet; toss to coat. Reduce heat to medium; cook until heated through. Top with cheese.

Makes 3 to 4 servings

Tuna Ramen Casserole

  2   packages (3 ounces each) ramen noodles, any flavor, broken in half*
 ¾   cup broccoli florets
  1   can (about 5 ounces) tuna in water, drained and flaked
 ¾   cup (3 ounces) shredded Italian cheese blend, divided
 ½   cup milk
 ¼   cup mayonnaise
  1   teaspoon salt
 ¼   teaspoon red pepper flakes

*Discard seasoning packets.

1 Preheat oven to 350°F. Grease 8-inch glass baking dish.

2 Bring water to a boil in medium saucepan over medium heat. Boil noodles 1 minute. Add broccoli florets. Boil noodles and broccoli 1 minute more. Drain and rinse with cold water.

3 Combine tuna, ½ cup cheese, milk, mayonnaise, salt and red pepper flakes in large bowl. Stir in noodles and broccoli. Spread in prepared dish. Top with remaining ¼ cup cheese blend.

4 Bake 15 minutes or until cheese is melted.

Makes 2 to 3 servings

 Tip:

Adding broccoli and cheese to your tuna casserole makes this an all-in-one meal.

Quick & Easy Chicken Pesto Salad

1   package (3 ounces) ramen noodles, any flavor, broken into 4 large chunks*

1   cup chopped cooked chicken

½   cup halved grape tomatoes

¼   cup slivered or finely chopped carrots

1   to 2 tablespoons prepared pesto

      Salt and black pepper

Discard seasoning packet.

1 Bring water to a boil in medium saucepan. Boil noodles 2 minutes. Drain and rinse with cold water.

2 Combine noodles, chicken, tomatoes, carrots and pesto in large bowl; toss to coat. Season with salt and pepper.

Makes 2 servings

Ramen Pizza Pie

2	packages (3 ounces each) ramen noodles, any flavor*
2	eggs, lightly beaten
¼	cup milk
¼	teaspoon salt
1	cup ricotta cheese
1	cup pasta sauce**
1	cup (4 ounces) shredded part-skim mozzarella cheese

*Discard seasoning packets.

**For added flavor, choose a tomato-basil flavored sauce.

1 Preheat oven to 425°F. Grease a 9-inch pie pan. Cook and drain noodles according to package directions.

2 Whisk eggs, milk and salt in large bowl. Stir in noodles; toss to coat. Spread evenly in bottom of prepared pan. Bake 10 minutes or until set.

3 Top crust with ricotta, pasta sauce and mozzarella cheese. Bake 15 minutes or until cheese is melted and golden brown. Let stand 5 minutes before serving.

Makes 6 servings

Presto Pesto

1	package (3 ounces) ramen noodles, any flavor, broken in half*
1	tablespoon prepared pesto sauce
2	teaspoons pine nuts, toasted
5	grape tomatoes, halved
	Salt

*Discard seasoning packet.

Cook noodles according to package directions; drain well. Combine noodles and pesto sauce in medium bowl. Add pine nuts, tomatoes and salt; toss to coat.

Makes 1 serving

Fast Food Fares

RAMEN PIZZA PIE

Ramen Pepperoni & Cheese Casserole

- **2**   tablespoons unsalted butter, divided
- **1**   cup panko bread crumbs
- **½**   teaspoon plus ⅛ teaspoon salt, divided
- **4**   packages (3 ounces each) ramen noodles, any flavor, broken into chunks*
- **30**   pepperoni slices
- **1½**   cups pasta sauce
- **1**   tablespoon all-purpose flour
- **1½**   cups milk
- **¼**   teaspoon black pepper
- **½**   teaspoon dried Italian herbs
- **2**   cups shredded sharp Cheddar cheese, divided
- **1**   cup shredded mozzarella cheese

Discard seasoning packets.

1 Preheat oven to 400°F. Grease 13×9-inch baking dish.

2 Melt 1 tablespoon butter in large skillet over medium heat. Add panko and ⅛ teaspoon salt; cook 6 minutes or until lightly toasted, stirring occasionally. Transfer to small bowl.

3 Cook noodles according to package directions. Drain and rinse with cold water. Transfer to large bowl.

4 Place pepperoni on microwavable plate; microwave on HIGH 1 minute. Blot grease with paper towels. Add half of the pepperoni and pasta sauce to noodles.

5 Melt remaining 1 tablespoon butter in skillet over medium heat. Add flour; cook 1 minute. Add milk, remaining salt, pepper and Italian herbs; cook and stir 4 minutes or until thickened. Remove from heat; stir in 1½ cups Cheddar and mozzarella cheeses until melted. Add to ramen mixture; stir until noodles are evenly coated. Transfer to prepared dish.

Fast Food Fares

6 Sprinkle with remaining Cheddar cheese, pepperoni and panko. Bake 35 to 40 minutes or until bubbly and cheese is golden. Let stand 5 minutes before serving.

Makes 6 to 8 servings

Shrimp Ramen Pad Thai

7¼	cups water, divided
3	packages (3 ounces each) ramen noodles, any flavor*
4	tablespoons vegetable oil, divided
3	tablespoons packed light brown sugar
3	tablespoons soy sauce
2	tablespoons lime juice
1	tablespoon anchovy paste
2	eggs, lightly beaten
12	ounces medium shrimp, peeled and deveined
2	cloves garlic, minced
1	tablespoon paprika
¼	to ½ teaspoon ground red pepper
8	ounces fresh bean sprouts, divided
½	cup coarsely chopped unsalted dry-roasted peanuts
4	green onions with tops, cut into 1-inch lengths
½	lime, cut lengthwise into 4 wedges (optional)

Discard seasoning packets.

1 Place 6 cups water in wok; bring to a boil over high heat. Add noodles; cook 2 minutes or until tender but still firm, stirring frequently. Drain and rinse under cold running water to stop cooking. Drain again and place noodles in large bowl. Add 1 tablespoon oil; toss lightly to coat. Set aside.

2 Combine remaining 1¼ cups water, brown sugar, soy sauce, lime juice and anchovy paste in small bowl; set aside.

3 Heat wok over medium heat about 30 seconds or until hot. Drizzle 1 tablespoon oil into wok; heat 15 seconds. Add eggs; cook 1 minute or just until set on bottom. Turn eggs over; stir to scramble until cooked but not dry. Transfer to medium bowl; set aside.

Fast Food Fares

4 Heat wok over high heat until hot. Drizzle 1 tablespoon oil into wok and heat 15 seconds. Add shrimp and garlic; stir-fry 2 minutes or until shrimp begin to turn pink and opaque. Add shrimp to eggs.

5 Heat wok over medium heat until hot. Drizzle remaining 1 tablespoon oil into wok and heat 15 seconds. Stir in paprika and red pepper. Add cooked noodles and anchovy mixture; cook and stir about 5 minutes or until noodles are softened. Stir in three-fourths of bean sprouts. Add peanuts and green onions; toss and cook about 1 minute or until onions begin to wilt.

6 Add eggs and shrimp; stir-fry until heated through. Transfer to serving plate and garnish with remaining bean sprouts and lime wedges. Sprinkle with additional chopped peanuts, if desired.

Makes 4 servings

Crunchy Salmon Patties

  1   **package (3 ounces) oriental ramen noodles**

 ¼   **cup all-purpose flour**

  2   **cans (6 ounces each) pink salmon, drained and flaked**

 ¼   **cup finely diced onion**

 ¼   **cup finely diced red bell pepper**

  2   **eggs, lightly beaten**

  2   **tablespoons vegetable oil**

1 Place noodles, flour and seasoning packet in food processor; process until noodles become finely chopped.

2 Place salmon, onion, bell pepper and half of noodle mixture in large bowl; mix well. Add eggs; stir to combine.

3 Place remaining noodle mixture on plate. Form salmon mixture into 8 patties. Press both sides of patties into noodle mixture.

4 Heat oil in large skillet over medium-high heat. Cook patties in batches 3 to 5 minutes per side or until golden brown.

Makes 8 patties

Tip:

Try these patties with tartar sauce, sweet and sour sauce or Asian spicy mustard.

Ramen "Spaghetti" Tacos

 2   packets (3 ounces each) ramen noodles, any flavor*

 1   cup pasta sauce

 8   hard taco shells

 ½   cup grated mozzarella cheese

 ¼   cup shredded Cheddar cheese

       Chopped tomatoes

Discard seasoning packets.

1 Cook noodles according to package directions. Drain; return to saucepan. Add pasta sauce. Cook over medium heat until heated throughout.

2 Divide noodles evenly among taco shells. Top each taco with mozzarella and Cheddar cheeses. Microwave on HIGH at 10- to 15-second intervals until cheese is melted, if desired. Top with tomatoes.

Makes 4 servings

  Tip:

These tacos can be flavored in a variety of ways. Try them with salsa instead of pasta sauce and toppings such as sour cream, guacamole, shredded lettuce and grated Mexican cheese. Or, mix cooked noodles with teriyaki sauce and top with shredded cabbage, water chestnuts, bamboo shoots and chicken or pork.

Ramen Alfredo

- 1   cup whipping cream
- ¼   teaspoon salt
- ¼   teaspoon black pepper
- ⅛   teaspoon nutmeg
- 3   packages (3 ounces each) ramen noodles, any flavor*
- ½   cup grated Parmesan cheese, plus additional for garnish

Discard seasoning packets.

1 Combine cream, salt, pepper and nutmeg in large saucepan; cook over medium heat 8 minutes or until reduced to ½ cup, stirring occasionally.

2 Bring large saucepan of water to a boil. Add noodles; cook 1 minute. Drain noodles, reserving ¼ cup cooking water.

3 Add reserved cooking water and ½ cheese to cream mixture; bring to a simmer over medium-high heat. Reduce heat to medium-low; add noodles, tossing to coat. Cook 1 minute or until noodles are al dente and cheese is melted. Sprinkle with additional cheese.

Makes 3 servings

Tip:

Make Chicken Alfredo by adding chopped cooked chicken to this dish.

Peanut Noodles

3   tablespoons vegetable oil, divided

2   tablespoons peanut butter

1   tablespoon teriyaki sauce

    Juice of 1 lime

1   teaspoon chili-garlic paste (optional)

2   packages (3 ounces each) ramen noodles, any flavor*

¾   cup shelled edamame, thawed if frozen

½   cup thinly sliced red bell pepper

    Crushed peanuts (optional)

Discard seasoning packets.

1 Combine 2 tablespoons oil, peanut butter, teriyaki sauce, lime juice and chili-garlic paste, if desired, in large bowl.

2 Bring water to a boil in medium saucepan over medium-high heat. Add noodles and edamame; boil 2 minutes. Drain and rinse with cold water. Toss with remaining 1 tablespoon oil.

3 Combine noodle mixture and bell pepper with peanut butter mixture; toss to coat. Top with peanuts, if desired.

Makes 4 servings

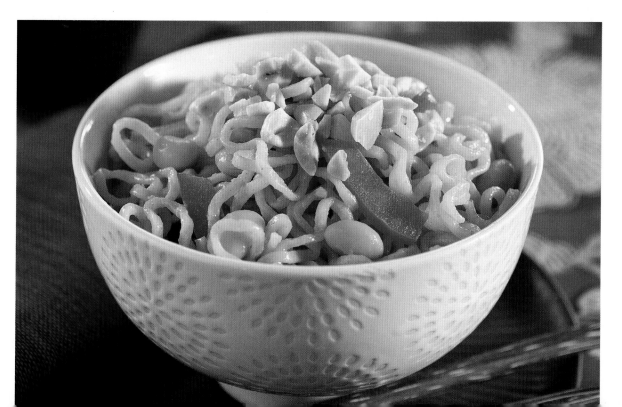

Crunchy Munchies

Rocky Road Bundles

- 1 cup semisweet chocolate chips
- ½ cup creamy peanut butter
- 1 package (3 ounces) ramen noodles, any flavor, broken into bite-size pieces*
- 1 cup mini marshmallows

Discard seasoning packet.

1 Combine chocolate chips and peanut butter in microwavable bowl. Microwave on MEDIUM (50%) 1 minute; stir. Repeat if necessary, stirring after 15-second intervals, until chocolate is melted and mixture is well blended.

2 Add noodles and marshmallows; mix well. Drop by tablespoonfuls onto baking sheet lined with waxed paper; refrigerate 1 hour or until firm.

Makes 1 dozen treats

Crunchy Munchies

Chocolate Ramen Fudge

1 package (12 ounces) semisweet chocolate chips

1 can (14 ounces) sweetened condensed milk

1 package (3 ounces) ramen noodles, any flavor, broken into bite-size pieces*

2 tablespoons butter, softened

1 teaspoon vanilla

Discard seasoning packet.

1 Line 8-inch square baking pan with foil, extending foil over edges of pan.

2 Place chocolate chips in medium microwavable bowl. Microwave on HIGH 1 minute; stir. Repeat, if necessary, for 30-second intervals, stirring after each, until completely melted. Mix in sweetened condensed milk, noodles, butter and vanilla.

3 Transfer mixture into prepared pan; spread evenly. Refrigerate 1 hour or until firm. Remove from pan; peel off foil. Cut into squares.

Makes 18 servings

Crunchy Munchies

Salad Crunchies

1 **package (3 ounces) ramen noodles**

⅓ **cup sesame seeds (about 1½ ounces)**

¾ **cup roasted, unsalted cashew pieces (about 4 ounces)**

1 Preheat oven to 350°F. Line baking sheet with foil. Set aside.

2 Remove noodles from package. Reserve seasoning packet for another use. Break noodles into pieces onto prepared baking sheet. Spread out in single layer. Sprinkle sesame seeds evenly over noodle pieces.

3 Bake 4 to 6 minutes or until sesame seeds are golden and fragrant, stirring once. Remove baking sheet from oven. Cool noodle mixture.

4 Combine noodle mixture and cashew pieces in mixing bowl. Transfer mixture to 1-pint wide-mouth jar. Seal jar until ready to use.

5 Sprinkle Salad Crunchies on any salad for a crunchy, nutty flavor topping. It's also great as a snack.

Makes 1 (1-pint) jar

Quick Oriental Chicken Salad: Purchase a roasted chicken, a bag of salad greens, a can of mandarin oranges, green onions and a bottle of Oriental salad dressing. Combine bag of salad greens with ½ to 1 cup shredded chicken. Add drained mandarin oranges and sliced green onions. Toss with dressing and top with Salad Crunchies.

Open-Faced "S'Mores"

1   package (3 ounces) ramen noodles, any flavor*
2   chocolate bars (1.5 ounces each), broken into sections
4   large marshmallows, halved

Discard seasoning packet.

1 Cut noodles in half horizontally with serrated knife, to make 2 squares. Cut each square in half crosswise, making 4 rectangles in total.

2 Divide chocolate pieces evenly over each rectangle. Heat in microwave on HIGH 10 seconds. Continue to microwave at 10-second intervals until chocolate just begins to melt.

3 Top each noodle square with 2 halves of marshmallows. Return to microwave 15 seconds or until marshmallows are puffed.

Makes 4 s'mores

 Tip:

The marshmallows can be toasted on a skewer over medium-high flame on the stovetop, if desired. You can also substitute hazelnut chocolate spread for the chocolate bars; if so, omit step 2.

Crunchy Munchies

Glazed Noodle Crunch

¼ cup (½ stick) butter, cut into small pieces

½ cup packed light brown sugar

½ teaspoon cinnamon

1 package (3 ounces) ramen noodles, any flavor, broken into bite-size pieces*

1 cup pretzels, broken into pieces

1 cup salted peanuts

½ cup dried cranberries

*Discard seasoning packet.

Melt butter in medium microwavable bowl on HIGH 30 seconds. Stir in brown sugar and cinnamon; microwave 1½ minutes, stirring after first minute. Stir in noodles. Spread mixture on waxed paper; cool completely. Place in large bowl; toss with pretzels, peanuts and cranberries.

Makes 4 cups

 Tip:

Add ½ cup semisweet chocolate chips to the mixture for additional color and sweetness.

Index

Acknowledgments

The publisher would like to thank the companies and organizations listed below for the use of their recipes and photos in this publication.

Campbell Soup Company
National Sunflower Association
Reckitt Benckiser LLC.
StarKist®